500 POSITIVE AFFIRMATIONS FOR BLACK WOMEN

Inspirational Thoughts to Boost Confidence and Motivation, Attract Love, Money and Success, and Manifest a Better Life

Alyssa Carter

Uranus Publishing

ISBN 978-1915218193

First Edition: March 2022

All rights reserved - © 2022 by Alyssa Carter

This book is copyright protected. It is only for personal use. The content of this book may not be reproduced, duplicated or transmitted without direct written permission from the author or the publisher. All pictures contained in this book come from the publisher's archive or copyright-free stock websites.

<u>Disclaimer Notice:</u>

Please note the information contained within this document is for educational and entertainment purposes only. All effort has been executed to present accurate, up-to-date, reliable, complete information. No warranties of any kind are declared or implied. Readers acknowledge that the author is not engaged in rendering legal, financial, medical or professional advice. The content within this book has been derived from various sources. Please consult a licensed professional before attempting any techniques outlined in this book. By reading this document, the reader agrees that under no circumstances is the author responsible for any losses, direct or indirect, that are incurred as a result of the use of the information contained within this document, including, but not limited to, errors, omissions, or inaccuracies. The trademarks used are without any consent, and the publication of the trademark is without permission or backing by the trademark owner. All trademarks and brands within this book are for clarifying purposes only and are owned by the owners themselves, not affiliated with this document.

TABLE OF CONTENTS

About Courage	1
Introduction	3
1. Self-Love	7
2. Self-Confidence	27
3. Self-Compassion	33
4. Mindfulness	45
5. Gratitude	53
6. Motivation	63
7. Abundance	69
8. Success	75
9. Forgiveness	85
10. Body Positivity	93
11. Love and Relationship	105
About Beauty	115

"Courage is the most important of all the virtues because, without courage, you can't practice any other virtue consistently."

— Maya Angelou

INTRODUCTION

As black women, our confidence, self-esteem, skills, and qualities are constantly challenged by society due to our race and gender.

Knowing this, it becomes a priority to uplift ourselves and identify with affirmations. We must utilize repetition to reprogram our subconscious mind and replace old and destructive beliefs with new and good ones corresponding to our aims and desires. You just have one moment to live, and that is all that matters. You have influence over the present moment, and if you don't choose to feel good about it, how will you construct a future that you will love and be pleased with? What kinds of thoughts do you have that make you feel good? Are they feelings of gratitude, love, joy, admiration, or childhood memories? Are you currently savoring the present moment and anticipating what's to come?

Having positive thoughts is an act of self-love, and loving yourself will allow you to experience miracles in your life.

What is an affirmation?

An affirmation is usually a sentence of powerful words strung together in the form of a positive statement, and this sentence is meant to, consciously or unconsciously, motivate, challenge, and push you to realize your greatest potential in life. In fact, every word you say and every idea you have is an affirmation. All of our internal discourse, or self-talk, is a stream of affirmations. Whether you realize it or not, you're using affirmations all the time. With every word and thought, you're validating and constructing your life experiences.

Interestingly, positive affirmations, whether repeated or chanted to ourselves, have the capacity to affect the way we think and act in our lives in a good way. They can even modify our emotions, alter our behaviors, and rethink our beliefs. Finally, they can assist us in achieving our life goals and reaching greatness.

How can positive affirmations be so life-changing?

The advantages of affirmations are numerous; they have assisted countless people all over the world in achieving great things, but more importantly, they can assist you in making positive life changes. I personally have always written the affirmations that I needed to see or repeat to myself and stuck them on my wall so that they'd be the first thing that I see in the morning and the last thing that I see before going to bed, and they worked wonders!

Affirmations have always helped me through my hard times whenever I needed something positive to move forward, whenever I needed to regain my motivation to reach a goal or whenever I felt disappointed or disheartened in life. There were times when I had to study hard for very important exams, and I didn't have anyone to support or motivate me. I wrote things for myself that I needed to hear from a loved one, which actually never happened. Those positive affirmations that were always on my wall above my head did help me. They actually did change my attitude and mindset toward success, consistency, perseverance, my body image and even my relationships. Those affirmations helped me go forward and continue fighting for my life despite all the hardships and trauma happening around me, whether at home or at college. They truly did help me stay motivated and even survive the hard times!

As you see in my own story, affirmations have the power to motivate you to do certain things, to focus on achieving your life goals, to change your negative thinking patterns and replace them with positive thinking patterns. They also assist you in accessing a new belief system and, most importantly, reaffirm positivity in your life and help you regain or increase your self-confidence. You must repeat the affirmation on a daily basis and sincerely believe in the things you are saying to be effective.

This book is a collection of the most effective affirmations for those who want to make positive changes in every aspect of their life. I recommend you to use affirmations wisely since they are a powerful and life-changing tool. Are you ready for the flow of positivity, success, abundance and happiness pouring into your life? Let's get started then!

CHAPTER 1
SELF-LOVE

Self-love involves your ideas and feelings about yourself, as well as how you treat yourself. So, when you think of self-love, try to imagine what you'd do for yourself, how you'd talk to yourself, and how you'd feel about yourself if you loved and cared about yourself.

When you love yourself, you have a good outlook on life. This does not imply that you always feel good about yourself. That would be impossible! For example, I can be sad, furious, or disappointed with myself for a short period of time and yet love myself. Consider how this works in other relationships if this is unclear. Even when I'm furious or frustrated with my younger sister, I can still love her. My affection for her informs how I interact with her, even in the midst of my anger and disappointment. It enables me to forgive her and respect her. Self-love is pretty similar to that. That is to say, if you know how to love others, you can love yourself!

<u>What does it mean to love oneself?</u>

The following are some instances of how self-love can be manifested.

- Positive self-talk is a great way to start.
- Allowing yourself to be forgiven when you make a mistake
- Taking care of yourself
- Assertiveness
- Allowing no one to take advantage of you or exploit you
- Putting your health and well-being first
- Spending time with people who encourage you and help you grow (and avoiding people who don't)
- Requesting assistance
- Allowing yourself to let go of any grudges or animosity that is holding you back.
- Recognizing your abilities
- Putting your feelings first
- Choosing healthful food most of the time
- Living a life that is consistent with your ideals
- Pursuing your passions and objectives

- Putting yourself to the test
- Taking responsibility for your actions
- Providing oneself with nutritious delights
- Acceptance of your flaws
- Having reasonable expectations
- Observing and appreciating your efforts and development

<u>Why is it so important to love ourselves?</u>

If you didn't have any role models for self-love or anyone who told you how important it is to be good to yourself as a child, you could doubt its usefulness.

You're more prone to self-criticism and slip into people-pleasing and perfectionism if you don't love yourself. You're more prone to put up with other people's maltreatment or mistreatment. Because you don't value yourself, you may overlook your own wants and feelings. You might also self-destruct or make judgments that aren't in your best interests.

Self-love is the foundation for being assertive, setting boundaries and creating healthy relationships with others, practicing self-care, pursuing our interests and goals, and feeling proud of who we are.

Here are some powerful affirmations for Self Love that I provided for you. Repeat or chant them every day and every evening, making them part of your daily routine. I promise they will work wonders and will resonate with you soon.

Get started loving yourself and enjoy the process!

I love myself and everything about myself.

I love who I am.

I love all of me.

No one loves me the way I do.

I am deserving of love with all my flaws.

With love, I accept myself completely.

I unapologetically love myself.

∞

I am deserving of happiness.

∞

I respect my own boundaries.

∞

I am enough and worthy of love.

∞

Today, I choose myself.

∞

I adore the woman that I am.

∞

I am loved.

∞

I am deserving of love.

I am kind to myself.

Love flows from within me.

I treat myself with care and love.

I am lovely both inside and out.

I am entitled to joy.

I am whole because I let go of negative self-talk.

Everything I require is already within me.

I am in charge of my pleasure and capable of achieving my objectives.

∞

I accept myself totally.

∞

I don't allow my anxieties to hold me back.

∞

I'm glad for what I have, and I take care of myself.

∞

I love and accept myself completely.

∞

I am strong, and I am accomplished, so loving myself comes effortlessly to me.

∞

My ability to love myself is limitless.

∞

I let go of individuals who do not have my best interests at heart.

I am a work of art.

I am treasured.

I am so precious.

I allow myself to feel deeply.

I am receptive to love.

I adore myself as I am.

I have a warm and compassionate heart.

∽

I am exactly who I need to be right now.

∽

I send love to my anxieties and uncertainties.

∽

Negativity is repelled by me.

∽

I believe in myself.

∽

I can say no when something does not serve me.

∽

I can let go of what no longer serves me.

∽

I can easily accept compliments.

I am worthy of compliments.

I can let go of any need for suffering.

I have a lot to offer to the world.

I love every aspect of who I am.

The universe's loving energy surrounds me.

My life is full of love and happiness.

I have always done my best and will continue to do so.

I have accomplished wonderful things.

∽

I hold myself in high regard.

∽

My life is a place of harmony and balance.

∽

I choose to stop apologizing for who I am.

∽

My flaws or mistakes do not define me.

∽

Others accept and love me for who I am.

∽

I put myself first and foremost.

∽

I exude self-assurance.

My head is flooded with loving ideas.

I draw positive and loving people into my life as I practice loving myself.

The more I practice loving myself, the more likeable I become.

I let love in.

My love for myself grows each day.

I love myself more than ever.

I respect myself more than anybody else.

I honor and respect my own life path.

I honor and accept my limitations.

My life is a mirror of the love inside me.

I have a lot to love about myself.

I simply need my own approval since I exude love.

I enjoy loving myself.

I enjoy self-care.

I rejoice in loving the way I am.

∞

I don't need anyone's approval to feel worthy.

∞

I attract love and light to myself.

∞

I let go of the need to be critical of myself.

∞

I'm going to start loving myself more than ever today.

∞

I'm capable of loving myself fully and completely.

∞

I can take care of myself because I adore myself.

∞

My life is brimming with possibilities for achievement and happiness.

∞

My inner world shapes my outward environment, and I reward myself for my devotion and hard work.

∞

I am in a good place.

∞

The universe is always on my side.

∞

I have a positive relationship with myself.

∞

I choose to love and cherish myself instead of criticizing myself.

∞

I can love people more if I love myself more.

Loving myself is the best thing that can ever happen to me.

I have a positive and healing effect on others when I love myself.

I am my own healer.

I heal my soul with the great love I have for myself.

I see love in the mirror.

I am proud of myself when I choose to love myself.

Self-love is the best thing I can do for myself.

My dearest friend is my body, and I choose to nourish it.

I am the healer of my own sufferings, and I am love.

I have both strengths and flaws, just like everyone else.

No one is without flaws.

Every one of us is a work in progress.

I have faith in myself.

I am sufficient.

I'll be kind to myself as if I were my bestie.

I am a stunningly distinct individual.

I am proud of who I am.

I'm not scared of my emotions.

I'm exactly where I should be.

I shine like a diamond.

I'm not going to apologize for being myself.

I have a lot to be thankful for.

∞

I have faith in myself.

∞

I'm letting go of criticism and judgment.

∞

I am a gift to the rest of the planet.

∞

I'm capable of dealing with whatever that comes my way.

∞

I'm done with self-pity.

∞

I lavish compassion on myself.

∞

My relationship with myself is one that I treasure.

I am capable of accomplishing my objectives.

I have a lot to contribute.

I prefer to think positively.

I am aware of my limitations and grateful for the abilities I possess.

I love all about myself, the beautiful human being that I am.

CHAPTER 2
SELF-CONFIDENCE

Self-confidence is a mindset about one's own strengths and skills. It implies that you accept and trust yourself and are in command of your life. You have a good outlook on yourself and are aware of your strengths and weaknesses. You speak assertively, set realistic expectations and goals, and can handle criticism.

On the other side, low self-confidence might make you feel insecure, meek or submissive and make it difficult to trust people. You might feel unwanted, inferior, or sensitive to criticism. Whether or not you are self-assured depends on the situation. For example, you may be confident in some areas, such as academics, but not in others, such as relationships.

High or poor self-confidence is primarily based on your views rather than your real ability. Perceptions are how you think about yourself, and they might be inaccurate.

Low self-confidence can be caused by a variety of events, such as growing up in a judgmental and unsupportive environment, being separated from friends or family for the first time, evaluating yourself too harshly, or being terrified of failure. People with poor self-esteem frequently make logical blunders.

Here I've provided some positive affirmations for self-confidence. Repeat or chant them to yourself every day. Over time, you'll see that they are working in your conscious and unconscious, and you'll enjoy living with more self-confidence.

I choose to be confident today.

I choose to respect myself.

Every day, I am learning and growing.

∞

I have faith in myself and my abilities.

∞

I believe in myself.

∞

I have the power to overcome this difficult situation.

∞

I have the power to change my world.

∞

I am capable of completing any task.

∞

I can do anything I set my mind to.

∞

I am confident in my abilities.

∞

I grow with every challenge.

∞

I am consistent in my hard work.

∞

I know that hard work pays off and I'm confident I'll get the result I desire.

∞

I have everything I need to succeed.

∞

I let go of limiting my beliefs and choose to trust myself.

∞

My power is unlimited.

∞

I am proud of my culture and my upbringing.

∞

I am a strong confident black queen that deserve all the wonderful things in the world.

☙

I know I can face every challenge with ease, there is nothing I cannot overcome.

☙

I am creating my dream life every single day.

☙

I'm getting closer to my goals every day.

☙

I show up every day and do my best.

☙

I am in full control of my life.

☙

I release negative self-talk and choose to be more confident in myself.

I am comfortable in my own skin.

I believe in my abilities and express my true self with.

I choose to trust the process.

I am confident that I can do it.

Chapter 3
SELF-COMPASSION

Compassion for oneself is essentially the same as compassion for others. Consider how kindness makes you feel. To develop compassion for others, you must first recognize their suffering. You can't feel compassion for the homeless person on the street if you ignore them. Second, compassion entails being moved by others' grief to the point where your heart responds to it (compassion literally means "to suffer with"). When this happens, you feel a sense of warmth, compassion, and a desire to help the individual who is suffering. Compassion also entails treating others with empathy and kindness rather than harsh judgment when they fail or make mistakes. Finally, compassion (rather than pity) implies you recognize that suffering, failure, and imperfection are all part of the human experience. "If it weren't for luck, I'd be there."

When you're having a hard time, failing, or noticing something you don't like about yourself, self-compassion is acting the same way toward yourself. Instead of simply dismissing your discomfort with a stiff upper lip, you stop to think to yourself, "This is truly difficult right now," and ask yourself, "How can I soothe and care for myself at this moment?"

Self-compassion means you are compassionate and understanding when confronted with personal weaknesses, rather than harshly criticizing and blaming oneself for various inadequacies or flaws — after all, whoever said you were supposed to be perfect?

You may strive to change in ways that make you healthier and happier, but you are doing it because you care about yourself, not because you are worthless or unacceptably yourself. Most essential, having compassion for yourself involves respecting and accepting your humanity. Things will not always go your way. You will face frustrations, lose money, make blunders, reach your limits, and fall short of your goals. This is the human condition, which we all share.

Here I've provided some self-compassion affirmations which will definitely help you be more compassionate and understanding toward yourself. Include them in your daily routine and repeat or chant them to yourself in the morning and in the evening. They will regenerate some new pleasant changes in the way you treat yourself. Welcome to this wonderful world!

☙

I am ready and willing to put compassion into practice.

☙

I want to be more kind to myself.

☙

I am ready to give myself more understanding and compassion.

☙

I choose to be kind to myself.

☙

I trust myself and the path I've chosen.

☙

I deserve kindness.

☙

I deserve kind words.

∽

I want to stop criticizing myself and start celebrating myself.

∽

I don't want to ignore myself anymore.

∽

I do feel better one heartbeat at a time.

∽

I deserve to be treated with kindness.

∽

I deserve understanding.

∽

No one can be as kind to me as I am.

∽

My enthusiasm is fueled by self-compassion.

∽

I've come to discover the magnificence of my own existence.

∽

My bodily presence is reason to rejoice.

∽

I respond to discomfort by giving it my whole attention.

∽

I'm doing the best I can with what I've got.

∽

In this moment, I choose to be kind to me.

∽

Mistakes show that I'm growing and learning.

∽

I am deserving of affection because I value myself.

Taking time to heal is beneficial.

I am confident that I always give it my all.

God accepts me as I am.

God created me in the way that he did for a reason.

My flaws are my best friends because they teach me how to be a better person.

It's best for me to let go of what doesn't serve me anymore.

I'm a patient person when it comes to the process.

༄

My finest will suffice.

༄

I'm a person who lives with an open heart.

༄

I accept both my greatest and worst qualities.

༄

I am a soul on a wonderful adventure.

༄

It's never easy to change, but it's a lot simpler if I'm kind to myself.

༄

Love is the source of my existence.

༄

It's fine for me to be kind to myself.

Respect begins with love, so I love myself completely.

My ego does not define me. Love is what makes me who I am.

Love pours through my veins 24 hours a day, 7 days a week.

"Me time" is a healthy gift that I gratefully accept.

I accept myself as I am.

I am enough.

∽

I am worthy of compassion.

∽

I allow myself to make mistakes and to learn from those mistakes.

∽

My mistakes don't define me as a person.

∽

I am aware of my potential.

∽

The more compassionate I am with myself, the better I feel.

∽

I am capable of giving the kindness and love that I deserve.

∽

Like everyone else on the earth, I have strengths and

weaknesses, and that's OK.

∞

I want to heal through self-compassion.

∞

I deserve healing.

∞

Every action I perform is done with love for the glory of God.

∞

I'm a godsend.

∞

I deserve to be treated like a queen.

∞

My heart is in good hands.

∞

Love endures adversity because it is eternal.

I am a loving light entity.

I give myself the gift of unconditional kindness.

No one can take care of me as I do.

Inside of me, there is a loving light.

I have the freedom to make decisions that are best for me.

It is safe for me to be true to myself.

Love follows me everywhere.

I accept myself where I am right now.

∞

I love and accept myself as I am.

∞

I have the power to make myself feel loved and appreciated.

∞

I approve of myself wholeheartedly.

∞

I am becoming a better version of myself each day.

∞

I take care of my body and soul with kindness.

∞

CHAPTER 4
MINDFULNESS

Mindfulness is defined as "consciousness that occurs as a result of paying attention on purpose, in the present moment, and without judgment."

Psychologists define mindfulness as a "non-elaborative, nonjudgmental, present-centered awareness in which each thought, feeling, and experience that arises... is acknowledged and accepted as it is".

As simple as it may appear, mindfulness changes how we respond to events and experiences. It cultivates a more open, less reactive, and generally happier way of being in the world.

Consider your reaction when you don't believe you're good at something, such as completing brain teasers. So, what do you do when you're given a brain teaser? Do you tell yourself things like "I'm not very good at this," or "I'm going to look stupid"? Is this causing you to lose focus on the puzzle you're working on?

What if you approached the brain teaser with an open mind, unconcerned about your performance and simply curious about how it would go? What if you could directly experience the process as it unfolded—the problems, concerns, discoveries, and accomplishments—acknowledging and accepting each idea or feeling without having to figure it out or investigate it further?

When you do this frequently, you'll notice that you develop habitual patterns that cause you to react in negative or unhelpful ways, causing you more stress. You can gain a broader perspective and choose a more effective reaction by observing rather than responding.

Since mindfulness has helped me a lot in stress management and gave me the gift of being more calm and peaceful with people and the world around me, I've provided some mindfulness affirmations to help you observe yourself and the world around you without judgment or resentment. These affirmations will help you react less to all the noise around you and be more concentrated on yourself and the life you dream of. Rejoice in tranquility!

I am here.

∞

I am present.

∞

I am grounded.

∞

I am in here and now.

∞

At this moment, I have everything I need.

∞

I am exactly where I am meant to be.

∞

I am completely safe and secure right now.

∞

I am rooted in this present moment.

I am strong, steady, and grounded.

∞

I celebrate the present by being present only at this moment.

∞

I want to be only in the present moment.

∞

I exist at this moment right now.

∞

No matter what happened in the past, I want to be focused on this present moment.

∞

All I have is this present moment, and I'm happy about it.

∞

I am grateful for the breath that flows through my

lungs.

∞

My breath is my anchor.

∞

I am breathing in strength. I am breathing out peace.

∞

I feel peaceful, grounded, and secure.

∞

This moment is exactly as it's meant to be.

∞

I am experiencing life through all of my senses.

∞

I allow myself to focus on completing one step at a time.

∞

My power is in the present moment.

I am not my thoughts.

I am not my fears.

I am viewing the world through the eyes of love.

All is well at this moment.

My heart is grateful, and my mind is at peace.

I will not worry about things I cannot control.

I focus on what I can control and let go of what I cannot.

I have the power to overcome my doubts, worries, and fears.

∞

I allow myself to take things one moment at a time.

∞

I am grounded, centered, and stable.

∞

I know deep inner peace.

∞

This day is a gift, and I accept it with my full presence and undivided attention.

∞

I release worst-case scenario thinking and choose to focus on this present moment.

∞

When I'm feeling overwhelmed, I allow myself to step back and breathe.

I notice my thoughts and feelings without judgment or criticism.

Everything I feel in this moment is exactly right.

I take care of the future by taking care of the present moment.

I release my worries and allow myself to find peace in life's quiet moments.

Chapter 5
GRATITUDE

What exactly is gratitude?

Gratitude is a positive feeling that entails being grateful and thankful, and it has been linked to a variety of mental and physical health advantages. You feel grateful for something or someone in your life and respond with feelings of warmth, kindness and other forms of appreciation.

Depending on how and in what context people use it, gratitude can have a variety of connotations. However, Researchers believe that "gratitude stems from the recognition that something good has happened to you, accompanied by an appraisal that someone, whether another individual or an impersonal source, such as nature or a divine entity, was responsible for it."

How to Put Gratitude into Practice

Developing a sense of thankfulness isn't a difficult or challenging task. It doesn't necessitate any particular equipment or training. And the more you do it, the better you will get at it and the more appreciative you will be. Here's how you can do it:

Observe the situation: Take a moment to think about what you've just experienced and how you're feeling. Note of your senses and consider what is assisting you in coping. Are there individuals or things that have helped you manage your stress, feel good about your life, or accomplish what you need to do? Thank them with kindness.

Finally, repeat or chant the following affirmations I've collected for you. They help you acknowledge what you already have and be more appreciative of the blessings in your life.

I'm thankful for the life I've been given.

I'm honored to be a part of this incredible universe.

I am grateful for the blessings in my life, whether big or small.

∞

I am grateful for my family.

∞

I am grateful for my friends.

∞

I am grateful for having a place to stay and food to eat.

∞

I am grateful for being alive.

∞

I am grateful for breathing.

∞

I am grateful for being in this world.

∞

Every chance that comes my way makes me appreciative.

I am thankful for my freedom.

I am grateful for the natural beauty that surrounds me.

The sun, the moon, and the stars are all things for which I am grateful.

Every day, I am grateful to be able to count my blessings.

I'm thankful for the ability to offer and accept love.

Every day is a constant state of learning to me. Today, I am finding ways to be grateful for what I already have while also being excited for what is yet to come.

∞

I'm thankful that I can make a difference in the world.

∞

I am thankful for the small pleasures in life that make me happy.

∞

I am grateful for the ability to experience a wide range of wonderful emotions.

∞

I am thankful for all of the experiences I've experienced so far in my life.

∞

I'm thankful for all of the lovely places I've been throughout my life.

∞

Every day, I am grateful for the beauty that

surrounds me in nature. I do admit that I don't take enough time to appreciate everything, but that doesn't make my gratitude any less sincere.

∞

I am grateful for the opportunity to be myself.

∞

I truly appreciate all of the modern comforts that I have.

∞

The arms of abundance will be extended to me as long as I handle this situation with gratitude. I know I don't think about it every day, but I trust my spirit to lead me in the right direction.

∞

I am grateful for the opportunity to live.

∞

I am grateful for living in this modern world.

∞

I am grateful for being able to think.

I am grateful for being able to read.

∞

I am grateful for being able to see these beautiful words.

∞

I am grateful for my intelligence.

∞

I am grateful for being able to love.

∞

I am grateful to God for all these marvelous things around me.

∞

The more I notice everything in life that is working in my favor, the happier I am and the better my life gets every day.

∞

I am grateful to the universe for giving us humans such wonderful nature.

I'm grateful for being able to smile.

I am absolutely grateful for everything that has happened in my life so far and will wake up every day expressing this gratitude.

I know that everything will only continue to get better in my life. For that, I am very grateful.

I know that everything happens for a reason, I'm grateful for everything that has happened in my life so far.

I am truly grateful for the light that I see in the early morning. It gives me a sense of energy and strength to become the person I know I can be.

I'm grateful for the blue sky and the sunlight.

I am grateful for all the improvements I've made in my life.

I am grateful to myself as well for all the way I've come so far.

CHAPTER 6
MOTIVATION

What is motivation?

The drive to act in pursuit of a goal is known as motivation. It's the most important factor in determining and achieving our goals.

One of the driving elements underlying human behavior is motivation. It encourages competition while also encouraging social interaction. Its absence might result in mental diseases like depression. The desire to keep striving for meaning, purpose and a life worth living is referred to as motivation.

People may have many reasons for engaging in a particular behavior. Extrinsic motivation occurs when a person is motivated by external factors such as other people or prizes. Intrinsic motivation is when the inspiration comes from within—the drive to improve at a specific activity. Innate drive tends to push people harder, resulting in more satisfying outcomes.

The Maslow Hierarchy of Needs, created by American psychologist Abraham Maslow in 1943, is one paradigm for understanding motivation. According to Maslow, humans are naturally motivated to improve themselves and reach their full potential. It occurs by gradually encountering and satisfying various levels of need, ranging from the most basic, such as food and safety, to higher-order needs for love, belonging, and self-esteem.

What can I do to stay motivated?

Sometimes staying motivated every day becomes challenging, but I want you to know that it's normal to feel unmotivated at times. The action you can do is reading, repeating or chanting the affirmations I've collected for you to help you feel motivated again! Allow yourself to feel the discomfort, listen to the negative self-talk, and then take action nonetheless.

I am unstoppable.

I'm inspiring people through my work.

∞

I'm rising above the negative thoughts trying to make me angry or afraid.

∞

Today is a phenomenal day.

∞

Today is a beautiful day, and I'm going to make the most of it.

∞

I'm invincible.

∞

I can do anything I want to.

∞

I'm stronger than anything.

∞

I'm concentrated on achieving my goals.

I'm not allowing anyone to distract me.

I have a dream, and I'll do anything to make it come true.

Today is a productive day.

Today I choose to focus on my goals.

Today I'm going to be one step closer to my goals.

I win every single time.

I'm sure I'll achieve all my goals.

∞

I'm doing everything to make my dreams come true.

∞

I believe in myself, and I'll show it through my work.

∞

I'm constantly evolving into a better person.

∞

Today I'm not going to waste my time. I'm acting today.

∞

I've made it through hard times before, and I've always come out stronger and better. I'm going to make it through this as well.

∞

I must remember the incredible power I possess within me to achieve anything I dream of.

I don't have time to waste on negativity. I'm positive and motivated today.

I set goals and go after them with all my determination.

I'm determined to achieve my goals.

I have all the tools and abilities to achieve my goals.

I am sure that I can do it.

Note to self: I am going to make you so proud.

Chapter 7
ABUNDANCE

Let's try to define abundance and figure out what it means. The word originates from the Latin word 'abundantia.'

Plenty or a huge number of something is what plenty indicates. Nature and life have a natural will to manifest, grow, and become greater. The life force tends to produce and create more of everything. There are always new trees, plants, and fruits to be found. New products are continually being invented; new automobiles are being manufactured; new homes are being constructed, and new jobs are being created.

According to scientists, the universe is constantly expanding and evolving, and new stars are being formed. On a cosmic level, this is abundance. Abundance may be found all around the universe, and it can also be found in your personal life if you let it in. It takes the form of a plethora of trees, plants, animals, and various types of life, as well as an infinite number of stars and Universes. New stars are born every day, new plants are planted, new people are born, and new energy sources are discovered. The universe appears to be continually innovating. You are a part of this abundance. If you don't have enough in life, it's because negative thoughts and attitudes are preventing you from having it.

I'm here with a handful of affirmations for abundance, so it blooms in your life. Repeat them in the morning and evening, and an abundance of love, wealth, health, and friendship flow into your world!

I am worthy of what I desire.

I have everything I need to be successful.

I am grateful for the positive things in my life.

∞

I am open to limitless possibilities.

∞

I achieve whatever I set my mind to.

∞

I am smart, capable and talented.

∞

I am ready to share my gifts with the world.

∞

I surrender to the wisdom of the universe.

∞

I am my best source of motivation.

∞

I am creative and open to new solutions.

∞

I choose to embrace the mystery of life.

I choose faith over fear.

I allow everything to be as it is.

I attract miracles into my life.

I am attracting wealth and prosperity into my life.

I am open to receiving unexpected opportunities.

I am aligned with my purpose.

I am worthy of positive changes in my life.

I am grateful for the abundance that I have and the abundance that's on its way.

I am capable of achieving greatness.

I attract abundance.

The universe will give me whatever I desire.

My income increases constantly.

I choose to live a rich and full life.

I am ready to receive the abundance of all great things in my life.

CHAPTER 8
SUCCESS

Who doesn't want success in life? What do we mean by the word "success"? Success can be defined as accomplishments that make you feel fulfilled and satisfied with yourself. So, there is no fixed definition of success. It changes from person to person. There are also numerous strategies for achieving success in life, but your definition of success may determine the one that works best for you. We frequently associate it with performing well at work or earning significant pay.

While professional achievements are a significant part of life, they are only one piece of the picture. People might aim for success in various areas, including family, love relationships, academics, and athletics. Your definition of success may differ, but many people consider themselves successful if they are fulfilled, happy, safe, healthy, and loved.

It is the ability to achieve your life's objectives, whatever they may be. So, how can you improve your odds of accomplishing these goals? What are some of the successful people's habits?

Actually, there is no one-size-fits-all approach to success. It's possible that what works for you won't work for someone else. There may not be a perfect recipe for success, but with the psychological help of the affirmations for success and acting accordingly based on your definition of success, you can boost your chances of achieving it in life. The affirmations I've collected for you have always helped me stay motivated and charged with enthusiasm and strength in my hard times. So, remember to believe in yourself unconditionally, build a growth mindset and trust the process. Go get your goals!

I am succeeding in life.

Prosperity flows to and through me.

I will succeed by attracting people who can help me.

I want to maintain a positive attitude because I know it can help me achieve success.

I am full of vitality today. My confidence, positive attitude, and self-belief are my most valuable assets to take me a step closer to my success.

I am happy with who I am and who I can be.

Today, I will say goodbye to old bad habits and welcome a positive change into my life.

I am worthy enough to follow my dreams and manifest my desires.

Today I am prepared. I am prepared for success, love, happiness, peace, joy, and abundance! I am prepared for my wildest dreams to come true.

I am the architect of my fate. I can achieve what I have dreamed for myself.

I am stronger than all the challenges and hurdles lying in my way.

I am blessed to have everything in my life to make it successful.

I am attuned to the abundance of success.

I celebrate the abundance of everything in my life.

I believe I will succeed in getting all my goals.

I am open to receiving unexpected opportunities.

I am my best source of motivation.

I am capable of achieving greatness.

I attract miracles into my life.

I'm on the path to success.

I am open to limitless possibilities.

I continue to climb higher; there are no limits to what I can achieve.

I am a strong individual who attracts success and happiness.

I let go of old, negative beliefs that have stood in the way of my success.

The universe needs my light, and I am not afraid to shine.

Every day I become more powerful and successful.

I am worthy of all the good life offers, and I deserve to be successful.

I am always open-minded and eager to explore new paths to success.

I am a powerful creator. I create the life I want and enjoy it.

I am surrounded by positive, supportive people who believe in me.

∞

I stay focused on my vision and pursue my daily work with passion.

∞

I take pride in my ability to make worthwhile contributions to the world.

∞

Everywhere I look, I see prosperity coming into my life.

∞

As I allow more abundance into my life, more doors open for me.

∞

Wealth constantly flows into my life.

∞

My actions create constant wealth, prosperity, and

abundance

I am living my life in a state of complete abundance.

I believe that I can do anything.

I have goals and dreams that I am going to achieve.

I am a goal-getter and won't stop until I achieve my goals.

I am committed to achieving success in every area of my life.

I choose positivity.

I am worthy of my dream job and am creating the career of my dreams.

∞

I believe in me.

∞

I can accomplish all of my goals.

∞

I deserve success.

∞

CHAPTER 9
FORGIVENESS

What Is forgiveness and why is it important?

The act of forgiving others is known as liberating. It's the act of allowing oneself to be at peace with someone who has brought you to harm previously.

Here we want to look at the power of forgiveness and why it's so important to practice forgiveness toward ourselves and others.

Here are a few pointers to help you grasp the significance of forgiveness.

"Letting go of the hope that the past could have been any different" is one of the most realistic explanations of forgiveness I've ever heard.

It is just what it is. It was what it was. We can't undo what's happened, no matter how hard it is to accept or how desperately we want to change the past.

It has been proven that forgiveness improves mood, boosts optimism, and protects us against anger, stress, anxiety, and melancholy.

Stress hormones such as adrenaline and cortisol are released when the body carries the hurt or anger of an insult.

Eliminating the constant flow of those hormones also explains why forgiveness has physical health benefits, such as lowering the risk of hypertension and heart disease.

Holding on to previous hurts, anger, or resentment is like carrying a sack of heavy rocks around with you.

Every time you are insulted, another pebble is added to the bag. That idiot who cut you off on the interstate, there goes a pebble, your vexing coworker, a larger stone, your mother, who never loved you the way you deserved: another massive rock.

When someone "wrongs" us, we are naturally enraged, upset, and disappointed. A lot of the time, this feels justified. With the burdens of the past pulling us down, how could we ever move forward through forgiving ourselves and others? The following affirmations will help you forgive the past, release the pain, anger, hurt, and anxiety caused by the past events, heal emotionally and finally move on. Repeat them, write them on sticky notes, stick them to your wall, and chant them to yourself every morning and every evening. Believe me, forgiveness is the best gift you can give to yourself, so don't hesitate to stop holding onto the past and start forgiving today!

I lay down the burdens of doubt, shame, remorse, and humiliation.

I let go of the past to go forward with pure intentions.

I am capable of learning from my errors.

As I forgive myself, it becomes easier to forgive others.

I'm able to recover from the harm and pain I've inflicted.

I forgive my past mistakes.

I forgive everyone from my life in the past for my inner peace.

I forgive myself for not knowing what was best for me.

Whenever I make a mistake, I learn the lesson and move on.

I forgive myself a little every day.

I gradually release my body's grip on fury and rage.

∞

I forgive myself for too much involvement in the past and set it free.

∞

By recognizing my genuine past, I give up the hope of a different past.

∞

I exchange my hatred and anger for compassion and understanding.

∞

I acknowledge that I did the best I could with what I knew at the time.

∞

I have the courage to mend and reintegrate into society.

∞

Starting today, I will treat myself with respect and kindness.

I forgive others with the same ease, honesty, and loving compassion with which I forgive myself.

I take this modest step toward growth.

I forgive myself for holding a grudge against my parents. I realize that everybody makes mistakes. We are all human.

I am willing to accept myself completely.

I move with the flow of life's events.

I forgive my parents.

I forgive my friends.

I forgive myself for any regrets that I've been holding and instead want to focus on the present.

I forgive all the people who have done me wrong; I do it not for them but for my inner peace.

By forgiving myself, I become more patient and tolerant of others.

I choose to give up all self-criticism and self-sabotage.

I dissolve into an ocean of forgiveness and love.

As I forgive myself and move forward, I get stronger and better.

I forgive myself to regain my inner peace.

I can only share my blessings with the world if I forgive myself first.

Chapter 10
BODY POSITIVITY

What is body positivity, and why is it important?

Body positivity refers to the belief that all people deserve to have a positive body image, regardless of how society and popular culture perceive a particular body shape and size as ideal and perfect. Body positivity is about appreciating your current body and not berating yourself for changes that occur naturally as a result of aging, childbearing, or lifestyle choices. It also means feeling confident about your body, loving yourself and your body and ultimately accepting your body, in whatever shape and size.

However, body positivity is more than just questioning how society perceives people based on their size and shape. It acknowledges that judgments are frequently made based on color, gender, sexual orientation, and disability.

A secondary goal of body positivity is to assist people in realizing how popular media messages contribute to the relationship that people have with their bodies in terms of how they feel about food, exercise and clothing, and their health, identity, and self-care.

You can create a healthier and more friendly relationship with your body through the positive affirmations I've provided below. Remember! You are unique, you are one of a kind, and your body is your home forever. Love it and appreciate it as it deserves!

I love my body, and I love myself.

I am proud of everything about me.

I am a head turner.

I am perfect and complete just the way I am.

∞

I embrace my differences, because it is the differences that make me unique.

∞

I feed my body healthy and nourishing food and give it enough exercise because it deserves to be taken care of.

∞

I know the answers and solutions. I listen to my body and trust my inner judgment.

∞

My brain is the sexiest part of my body.

∞

My body is full of my awesomeness.

∞

I eat a variety of foods for my health, wellness and

enjoyment.

There is more to life than worrying about my weight. I'm ready to experience it.

Food is not good or bad. It has no moral significance. I can choose to be good or bad, and it has nothing to do with the number of calories or carbohydrates I eat.

Being grounded and whole makes me beautiful. I can get there just by being still, breathing, listening to my intuition, and doing what I can to be kind to myself and others.

I do deserve to be treated with love and respect.

My body deserves love.

My skin is as sweet as chocolate.

❦

I'm perfect the way I am.

❦

I look exactly the way I'm supposed to. I know it because this is the way God made me!

❦

It's not about working on myself; it's about being OK with who I already am.

❦

My body can do incredible things.

❦

My body is a gift. I choose to treat it with love and respect.

❦

My body is a miracle of the universe.

Life is too short and too precious to waste time obsessing about my body. I will take care of it to the best of my ability.

A weight goal is an arbitrary number; how I feel about myself is what really matters.

As long as I am kind to myself and think highly of myself, it doesn't matter what others think of me.

I trust the wisdom of my body.

I use my energy to pay attention to myself, my inner wisdom, virtues, path, and journey.

When I look to others to dictate who I should be or how I should look, I reject who I am.

Accepting myself as I am right now is the first step in growing and evolving.

All magazine photos are airbrushed, photoshopped, and distorted.

My body is a sacred love temple.

My body is a shining diamond.

I enjoy feeling good about my body.

I love all my curves, cuz curvy is sexy.

Being skinny or fat is not my identity. I am

identified by who I am on the inside, a loving, wonderful person.

My opinion of myself is the only one that counts.

My weight does not define me.

My existence makes the world a better place.

My well-being is the most important thing to me. I am responsible for taking care of myself.

No one has the power to make me feel bad about myself without my permission.

I don't let body shaming make me feel bad about my body. My body deserves love.

I eat for energy and nourishment.

I want to enjoy eating the foods that I make myself with love.

My body is precious.

My body is unique. It's only mine, and I take care of it.

My body is unique in its own way, and I adore it.

My body is a bikini body because I'm already sexy.

My needs are just as important as anyone else's.

I choose to stop comparing myself to other women, I am just special the way I am.

Chocolate (or fill in a food you have a challenging relationship with) is not the enemy. It's not my friend either. It's just chocolate, and it has no power over me.

Life doesn't start 10 pounds from now (fill in a number that's meaningful for you). It's already started. I make a choice to include myself in it.

Thighs, thank you for carrying me to where I want to go.

Belly, thank you for helping me digest.

Skin, thank you for protecting me.

❦

Other people don't dictate my choices for me, and I know what's best for myself.

❦

Taking care of my body feels fantastic.

❦

I choose to do and say kind things to and about my body.

❦

I don't have to look like anybody else to be beautiful. I am unique, and this is my power.

❦

My body is just excellent, and it deserves all the love, respect and care in the world.

Chapter 11
Love and Relationship

You've probably heard the saying, "Stop hunting for love, and you'll find it." But how do you find something that you're not specifically seeking? The solution is straightforward but nuanced: manifestation.

Rather than desperately searching for love, the concept of generating love proposes that you make room for it when you're secure and content with your existence without it. This is because the energy you exude eventually attracts you. And that at its most fundamental level is how you are going to manifest love.

When a person has loving thoughts and lives a loving life, the measurable vibration of love is a high frequency that can expand and increase. People are more inclined to respond to someone confident, loving, and compassionate with openness, friendliness, laughing, and joy. People are more likely to respond positively to someone who speaks and thinks positively. When someone makes the conscious decision to exclusively interact with others who have the same energy or vibe as them, they immediately eliminate negative, dark, or draining people from their lives.

This is regarded as "manifestation", but it's all about conscious living, which I describe as "living in your truth and accepting that what is appropriate for you will come to you.".

In this chapter, I've compiled a list of effective affirmations to help you attract love, improve your love life or strengthen your current relationship. Hope you rejoice in endless love!

Everywhere I go, I discover love.

I am deserving of love and affection.

I fully appreciate myself.

༺

I am a love magnet.

༺

I am deserving of a long-term, meaningful relationship.

༺

Love is all around me; it follows me wherever I go.

༺

My partner and I have a solid, loving, and committed relationship.

༺

Every day, my love for my partner grows stronger.

༺

Everywhere I go, I am showered with adoration.

༺

Every day, my boyfriend and I are completely in love with one other, and every day, my partner loves me.

∞

I'm surrounded by love.

∞

My middle name is Love.

∞

The power of love is within me, and I have the best partner on the planet.

∞

I attract lovely, loving, and kind individuals into my life by removing the internal barrier that keeps me from receiving love.

∞

With open arms, I welcome love into my life.

∞

I'm grateful to have caring people in my life, and I

value everything I have. I treat my relationship with the respect it deserves.

∞

Every day, I choose love and positivity.

∞

My spouse and I are completely devoted to one another, and we always have a good time together.

∞

My partner supports me in the same way that I support him.

∞

My spouse considers me to be everything they seek in a partner.

∞

My spouse and I are at ease and secure in each other's company. We laugh together every day, and I enjoy being intimate with him.

∞

My spouse is head over heels in love with me, and

I'm head over heels in love with my partner.

Our love is more powerful than disagreements and arguments.

Love triumphs between my partner and me, and I am ready and open to receiving love and blessings.

With open arms and an open heart, I welcome love.

I deserve an amazing love in my life.

My ideal partner is coming into my life, and I'm welcoming them.

I don't need to change anything to be fully loved and happy with myself.

I'm nice and attractive just the way I am. I'm content to be completely myself in the relationship without being unjustly criticized.

With the help of my loved ones, I get through life.

I've decided to love and approve of myself.

Now is the time for me to accept a positive, rewarding relationship.

My romantic relationship with my partner is ideal.

In my relationship, sensuality and romance are natural sentiments.

My romantic feelings are easily expressed to my spouse, and I am entirely open to receiving love.

∞

Love is drawn to me like a magnet because of my innate loving personality.

∞

My soul mate is my partner, and we love one other entirely and unreservedly.

∞

I've come to feel that partnerships may be both enjoyable.

∞

All of my relationships are now loving and harmonious, and I've let go of any sense of urgency to let love find me.

∞

The power of love is inside me.

∞

I naturally find love everywhere.

All eyes are on me wherever I go because I'm so loving and attractive.

"We delight in the beauty of the butterfly, but rarely admit the changes it has gone through to achieve that beauty."
— Maya Angelou

www.ingramcontent.com/pod-product-compliance
Lightning Source LLC
Chambersburg PA
CBHW071524080526
44588CB00011B/1551